To my beloved aunts, Bernadette Mosco and Mary McKercher. — RM

To my niece, Bianca, who makes me see the world with new eyes. — AP

Special thanks to Alex Wild for scientific advice.

Tundra Books, an imprint of Tundra Book Group,
a division of Penguin Random House of Canada Limited

Library and Archives Canada Cataloguing in Publication

Title: There are no ants in this book / written by Rosemary Mosco ; illustrated by Anna Pirolli.
Names: Mosco, Rosemary, author. | Pirolli, Anna, illustrator.
Identifiers: Canadiana (print) 20230466605 | Canadiana (ebook) 20230466613 |
ISBN 9781774881163 (hardcover) | ISBN 9781774881170 (EPUB)
Subjects: LCSH: Ants—Juvenile literature. | LCSH: Ants—Behavior—Juvenile literature. |
LCSH: Ants—Miscellanea—Juvenile literature. | LCGFT: Picture books.
Classification: LCC QL568.F7 M67 2024 | DDC j595.79/6—dc23

Published simultaneously in the United States of America by Tundra Books of Northern New York,
an imprint of Tundra Book Group, a division of Penguin Random House of Canada Limited

Library of Congress Control Number: 2023939514

Edited by Elizabeth Kribs
Designed by John Martz
The artwork in this book was created digitally.
The text was set in Gelica and Hupaisa.

Printed in China

www.penguinrandomhouse.ca

1 2 3 4 5   28 27 26 25 24

Penguin
Random House
tundra   TUNDRA BOOKS

There Are No Ants in This Book

WRITTEN BY **Rosemary Mosco**

ILLUSTRATED BY **Anna Pirolli**

tundra

What a nice-looking book this is!
It's the perfect place for . . .

. . . a picnic.

See, there are
no ants in this book.
It says so on the cover!
Ants love to eat picnic food,
and I do not want to share.

Yes, there are no ants here.
Zero.
Zip.
None.

Wrong! There's one!

Did you just hear
something?
It couldn't be.
It's . . .

I guess there is
one ant in this book.
But only one.

I AM A DINOSAUR ANT,
ONE OF THE LARGEST ANTS IN THE WORLD!
I'M AS BIG AS THIS STRAWBERRY!
THAT'S HUGE FOR AN ANT!

I am a **pharaoh ant,** and I'm only as long as six grains of salt. I'm one of the smallest ants in the world, but I dream big.

FINE. There are three ants in this book.
I'll be honest. This is more ants than I was expecting.
But three isn't a lot. Three ants can't eat
my whole picnic, right?

I'm a **winnow ant.** I gather flower seeds. I nibble on part of the seed and drop the rest to grow pretty flowers.
I'm a **honeypot ant.** I fill my big round butt with sweet sugar water. I store food in case my family gets hungry. I am a walking refrigerator!

I'm a **leafcutter ant,** and I'm a farmer. I cut pieces of leaf and take them home to feed the fungus that I eat.

ARRRGH!
I thought this was a book with no ants!
This book has the wrong title!
Somebody should fix it.
I can't believe there are
six ants in here!

I'm a **slender twig ant.** I live in a tree. If I fall off, I sail through the air and glide back to the tree, butt first. Whoosh!
I'm a **turtle ant.** I'm a living door. I use my big head to block the hole to my family's home and keep out any hungry bugs who want to eat us!

I'm a **green tree ant.**
I build a beautiful nest out of silk
and leaves for my family to live in.

I'm an **acrobat ant.**
If someone scares me,
I stick my butt high up in the air
and wave it around!

AAAAH!
Ten ants! TEN!
I'm shocked.
I'm stunned.
This is . . . This is . . .

This is COOL.
I didn't know there were so
many kinds of ants.
Big ants.
Small ants.
Ants with amazing butts.

I think I like ants.

That's good to know because most of us ants have . . .

...HUMONGOUS FAMILIES.

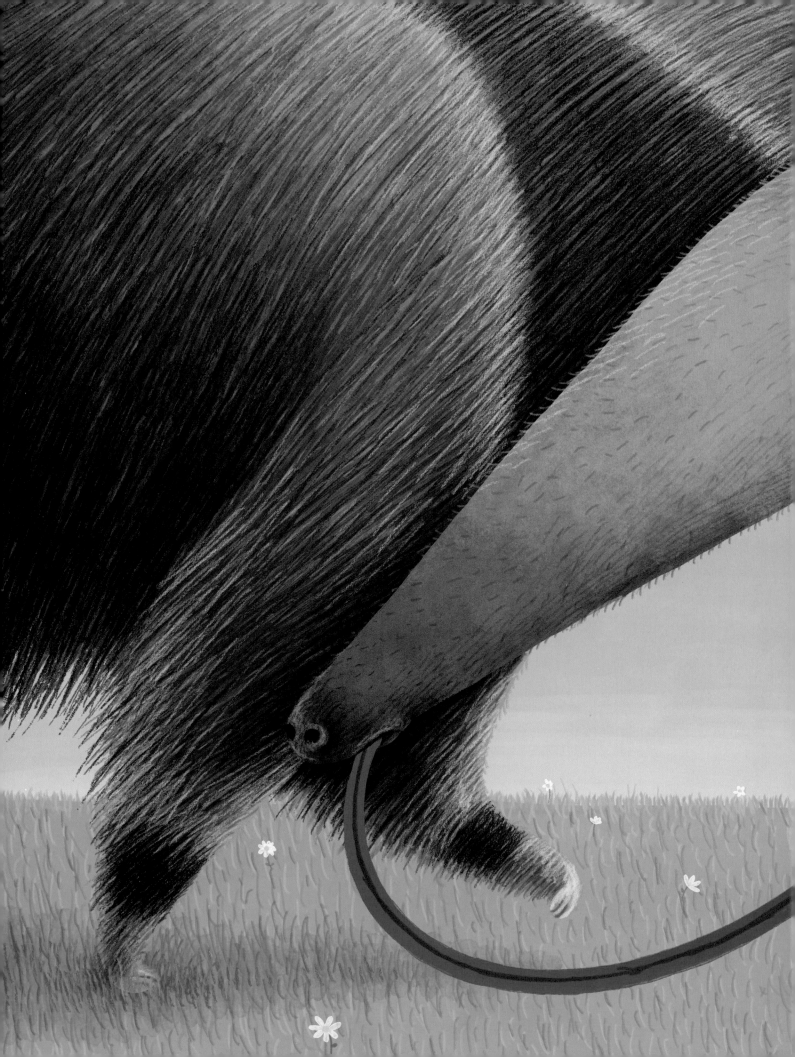

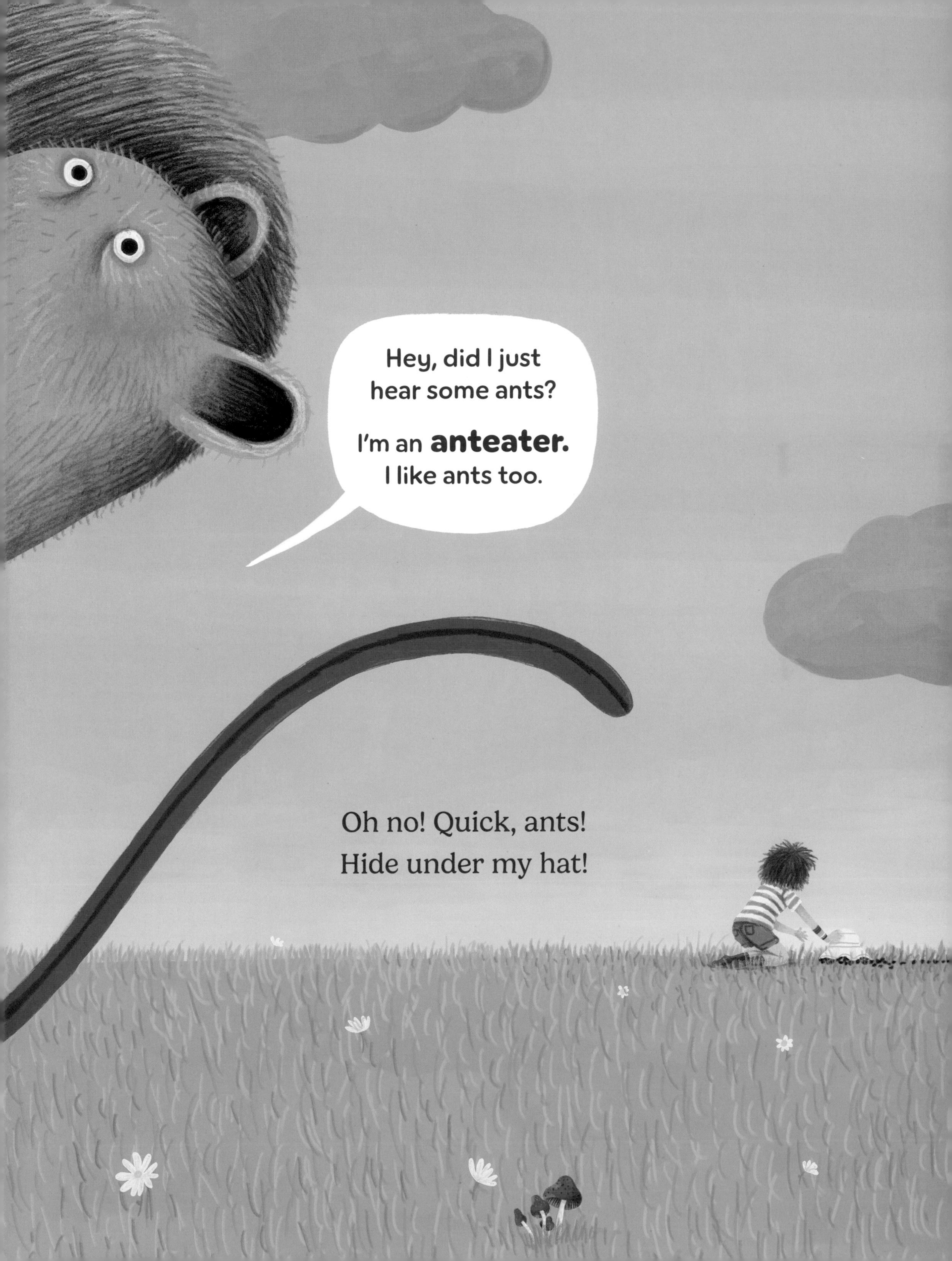

Oh no! Quick, ants!
Hide under my hat!

Didn't you read the title of this book?
There are no ants in this book.
Zero.
Zip.
None.

Didn't you read the title of this book?

It worked!
The anteater
is gone!

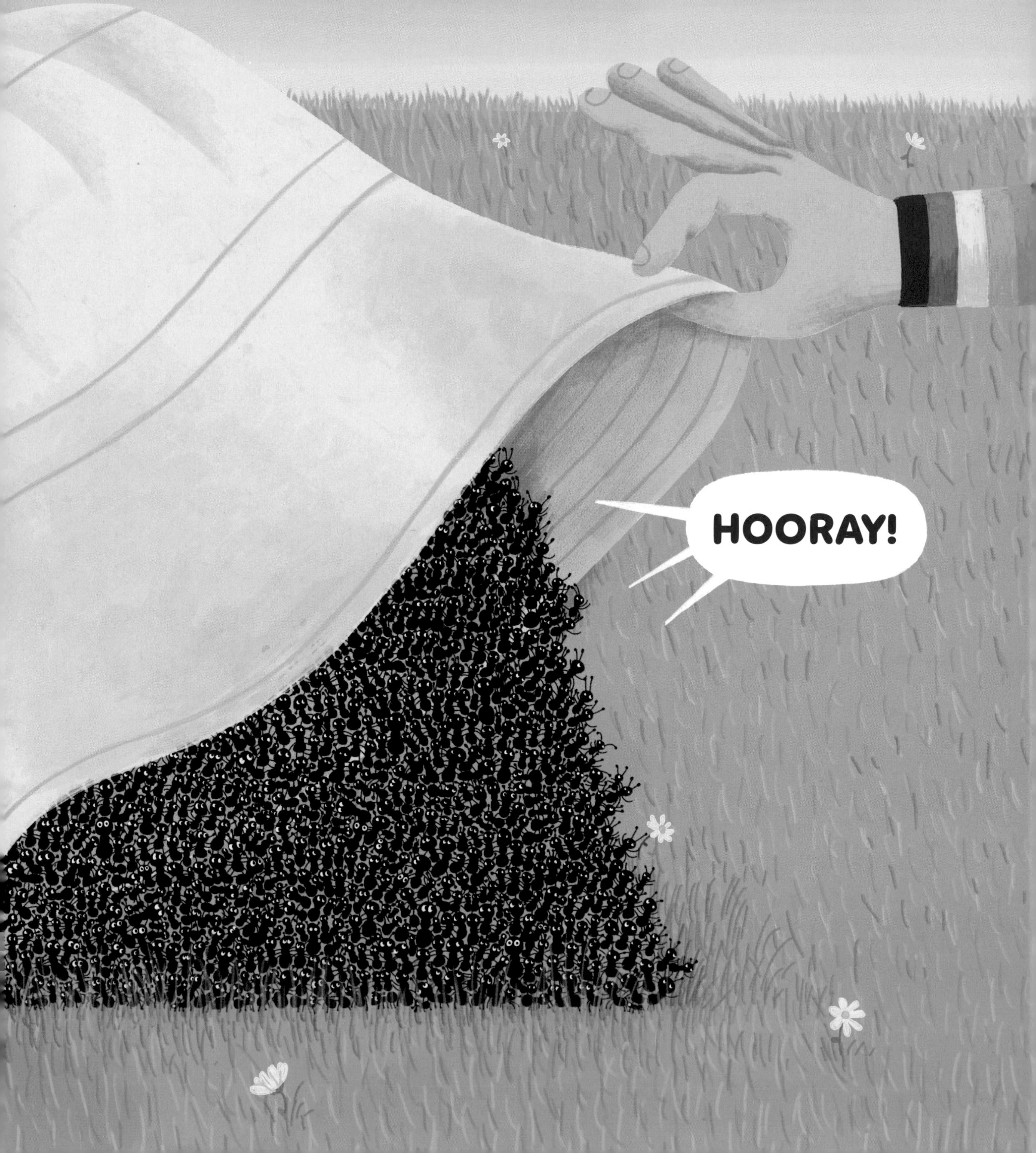

This book has the wrong title,
but I was right about one thing:
It's the perfect place for a picnic.

About the Ants in This Book

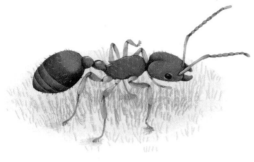

Acorn Ant *Temnothorax curvispinosus*

Where to find it: eastern North America

Ants live in groups called colonies made of dozens or even thousands of ants. The acorn ant's whole colony makes its home in small spaces such as an acorn, hickory nut or twig.

Dinosaur Ant *Dinoponera gigantea*

Where to find it: parts of South America

This gigantic ant searches for snacks on the forest floor. Like you, it eats all sorts of food. It loves fruits, seeds, mushrooms, insects and snails.

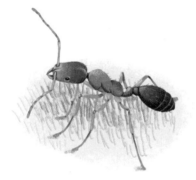

Pharaoh Ant *Monomorium pharaonis*

Where to find it: all over the world

The teeny tiny pharaoh ant loves making its home in buildings. It can squeeze through the smallest cracks to find crumbs of food that people have dropped.

Winnow Ant *Aphaenogaster rudis*

Where to find it: eastern North America

Some flower seeds have a part called an elaiosome, which ants love to eat. The winnow ant carries away the seed, eats the elaiosome and drops the rest to grow a new flower.

Honeypot Ant *Myrmecocystus mexicanus*

Where to find it: southwestern North America

Some honeypot ants fill their butts up with nectar and other food until they're huge. When food is scarce, they can use the nectar supply to feed their family members.

Leafcutter Ant *Atta cephalotes*
Where to find it: Mexico, Central America and South America

This ant is a farmer! It chews off pieces of leaf and carries them back to the large fungus farm in its underground nest. The fungus is the ant's only source of food.

Slender Twig Ant *Pseudomyrmex gracilis*
Where to find it: southern North America and South America

This ant lives high up in a tree. If it falls off, it can glide back to the tree's trunk, butt first! (The turtle ant can do this too.)

Turtle Ant *Cephalotes porrasi*
Where to find it: Mexico, Central America and northern South America

The turtle ant makes its home inside a hollow twig. Some members of its colony have special flat heads that they use to block the doorway to the twig and keep the nest safe.

Green Tree Ant *Oecophylla smaragdina*
Where to find it: southern Asia to Australia

Ants can be colorful. Some members of this species have emerald-colored butts. They make nests in trees by stitching leaves together with silk made by young ants.

Acrobat Ant *Crematogaster cerasi*
Where to find it: North America

The acrobat ant's butt, or "gaster," is heart shaped and oozes venom. When something spooks this ant, it waves its gaster and threatens to wipe a drop of venom onto its enemy. Ouch!

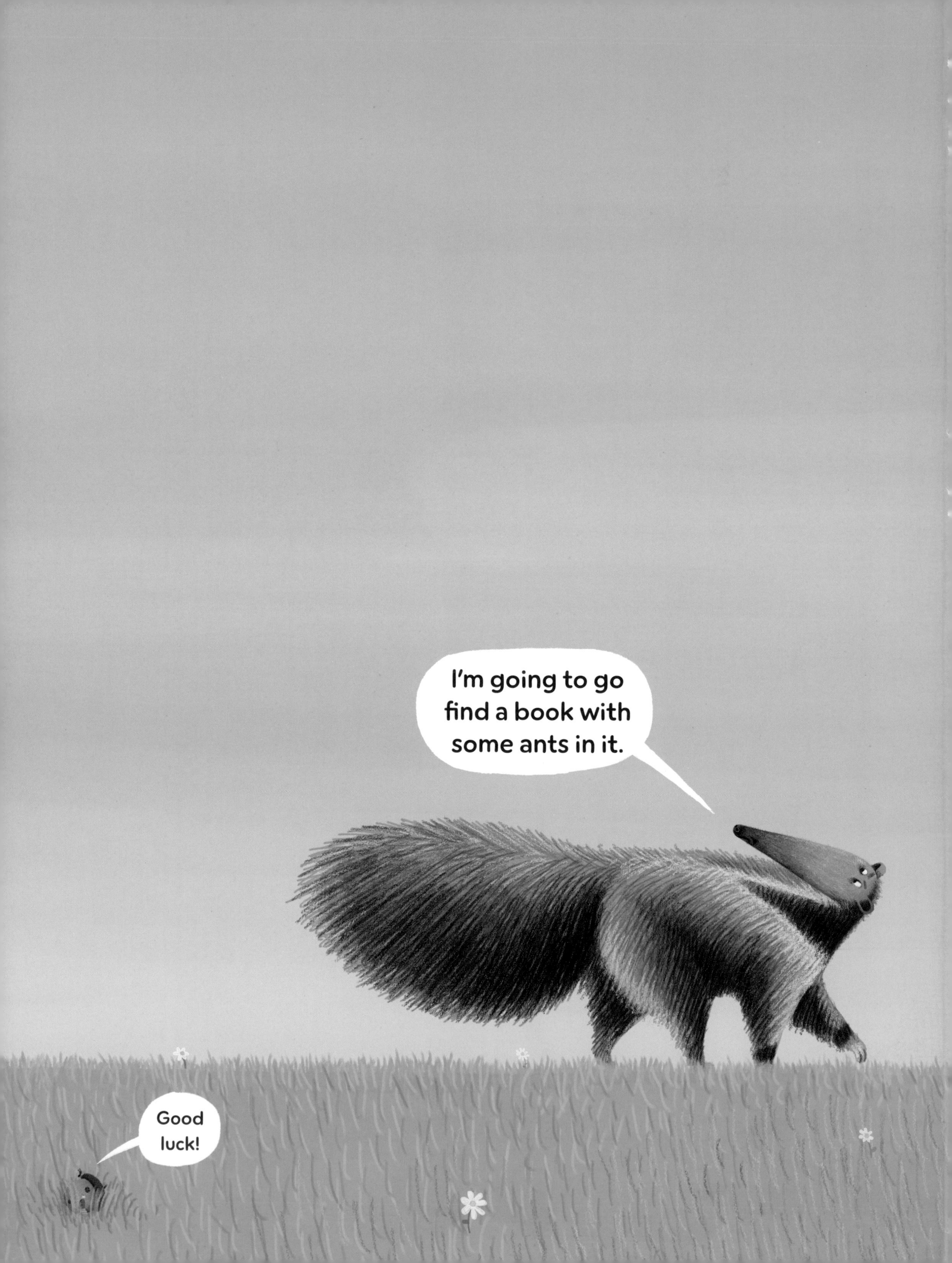
I'm going to go find a book with some ants in it.
Good luck!